The sayings of the Buddha

Reflections for every day

William Wray

SIRIUS

SIRIUS

This edition published in 2018 by Sirius Publishing, a division of
Arcturus Publishing Limited,
26/27 Bickels Yard, 151–153 Bermondsey Street,
London SE1 3HA

ISBN: 978-1-78888-335-1
AD006311UK

Printed in China

Contents

Introduction

Buddhism is considered to be one of the most important world faiths and it certainly has its influence on the spiritual life of the planet. It is estimated that half the countries of the world have been directly influenced by Buddhist thinking. How many practising Buddhists actually exist on the face of the globe is hard to estimate, but what is evident is that the power of Buddhism to capture the imagination of the human mind is as strong today as it was when the Buddha gave his doctrine of 'The Middle Way' to a gathering of five men who had been his original followers in the Deer Park in Saranath in about 450 BC.

This was a teaching that he himself thought long and hard about before delivering because he thought it so subtle and demanding that few would be able to follow, and yet, here in a time in which materialism is said to govern our thinking, the power of this man's spiritual realization still has a profound influence, and a growing one, particularly as far as the West is concerned. This says a lot about what this one man discovered in deep meditation. It also says a lot about us as human beings. Are his words of such forceful influence because they speak directly to something which all of us hold within us and in our more penetrating moments dimly realize?

An answer to this question can only be discovered if we devote time to a consideration of what he realized in his own life and sought to express in the years he spent teaching.

Arranged in the form of daily reflections, this book contains a range of aphorisms which express in different ways the core doctrines of Buddhism. They are derived mainly from the Pali Canon, written in the first century BC. This is a collection of manuscripts which recorded in writing the words of the Buddha that had previously been passed on orally. Also contained in the book are extracts of other works which hold a central position in the vast outpouring of the human spirit which constitutes Buddhist literature.

Life of the Buddha

S o what do we know about this man called the 'Buddha'? The first thing we have to realize is that this is not so much a name as an indication of his state of being. The Buddha is a title given to somebody of the highest spiritual understanding. It means 'One Who is Awake'. He is awake not in the way that we normally understand being awake. We are awake only to a dream of life within which we seek to create an identity. What this man was awake to was spiritual reality, things as they are in truth.

His name was Siddhartha Gautama. He was born in 487 BC in Lumbini, a state that spanned the border of modern-day Nepal and Northern India. He was born into the Kshatriya, the warrior caste, part of a ruling family. His father was determined to provide for his son: legend has it that Siddhartha was raised in a palace surrounded by high walls to prevent him from witnessing the suffering that is part of human experience.

His mother had a dream on conception that a white baby elephant entered her side. From this the seers predicted that Siddhartha would one day be either a great political or religious leader. We can only speculate as to whether or not his father was trying to shield him from the pain and suffering that can easily be central to the human lot. This seems likely, especially given that Siddhartha's own mother died when he was only seven days old. Another possibility is that in the light of the seers' prediction his father was concerned that one day Siddhartha would give up his privileged life and seek spiritual enlightenment as a way of transcending the sorrows of this world. Whatever the reason for his action, at the age of 29 Siddhartha slipped away in the night to become a wandering monk.

Before this Siddhartha had been raised with all the advantages his status in society was able to provide. At the age of 16 he was married to the beautiful Yahodra who bore him a son, Rahula. Despite the luxury of his life, this intelligent and sensitive man felt a lack; there was a spiritual understanding that wasn't available to him.

Later legend states that all of this came to a climax with four journeys he took out of the palace. On the first one of these, his father, determined to protect his son, arranged for the streets to be filled with happy and healthy people. He had all the old and infirm removed from view, but as chance would have it one remained undetected. When Siddhartha saw this, he commanded his charioteer to return to the palace in order to reflect upon what it meant to grow old. In his second journey he encountered a sick man and on the third a funeral procession. All this inevitably led him to ponder upon the transient nature of human existence, which no amount of privilege could protect him from. On his fourth journey he spoke to a holy man, a conversation which sowed in him the belief that it was possible to find a spiritual solution to what today we call existential misery.

Whether this legend is true or not, what is evident is that what he was facing in his life were the questions which we have all considered in some way. How do we find fulfilment in life? How do we overcome the pain that can so easily be our lot? What is the meaning of human existence and how might we discover the Truth? For Siddhartha, these questions were so pressing that he stole away in the middle of the night, left his family, his wife and child and renounced the world.

Wandering monks who had turned their back on worldly life were a familiar part of Indian life, as they are to this very day, in a land where schools of philosophy and gurus of various kinds abound. Siddhartha's first teacher, Ajara Kalama, taught him meditational techniques which encouraged ever deeper insight. His nature was such that he quickly mastered the techniques and achieved what was known as 'the sphere of nothingness'. Although such techniques granted more than a touch of bliss, the pain and suffering he encountered in the world as we know it remained regardless of the ease of mind discovered during meditation.

Siddhartha went on to study under Uddaka Ramaputta, who taught him techniques which allowed him to enter ever finer states, including the one described as 'the sphere of neither perception nor non-perception'. He recognized the validity of these states, but he also realized, sublime as they were, they were not what he was seeking.

After this he turned to austerity as a means of discovering that which he sought. He first developed breath control techniques which were based on reducing the intake of air, so much so that in practising these techniques it became possible to hardly breathe at all.

He then began reducing his intake of food. He carried this through until he was existing on one spoon of bean soup a day. For six years he practised these austerities, determined that through them he would achieve the enlightenment which he was seeking. What he discovered instead was that a life of extreme asceticism not only took its inevitable toll on his body but gave him nothing of what he was questing after. He came to the conclusion that rather than pursuing these extreme attempts to achieve realization, the only solution was to adopt what he came to describe as the 'Middle Way', neither over- indulgence nor self-mortification.

When he had come to this conclusion the small band of followers who had attached themselves to him over the years felt that he had turned his back on the path upon which they were depending upon him to lead them, and deserted him.

He was left to himself with no one to support him, his family gone, his followers gone, his reputation as man of insight and understanding ruined. Entirely alone, he was determined on one thing, the goal that he had always set himself: to cut through the maya, the veil of ignorance, and discover life's central reality, the source of true understanding.

It was at this point that a childhood memory came to mind. It was of his father ploughing whilst Siddhartha sat in the shade of a rose-apple tree. The steady measure of the ox-team, the play of sunlight and shade had allowed him so easily to slip below the surface of life and discover, unlooked for, what he now so desperately sought. Was 'Enlightenment' easy, so natural to man that it was child's play? Was he in all his desperate determination missing out on what was immediately to hand?

As this thought arose, he made up his mind that regardless of what was granted him, he would not take another step in this life until he found what he sought. He sat beneath a large, spreading tree and

entered into meditation. In the course of one night he achieved
the goal he had set himself, spiritual awakening. Having overcome
the force of worldly temptation, he, through contemplation,
obtained knowledge of the continual cycle of lives, not only those
that he had encountered personally but also the lives of all as
they rose and fell. He saw how people forged their own lives, of
how they were subject to their own actions. He saw the direct link
between craving and suffering. He saw his own identity dissolve
into the totality of being, the source of true understanding. In the
final watch of the night he attained full enlightenment. It was at
this point that Siddhartha Gautama became the Buddha. He
awoke from the dream of life and became enlightened.

For seven weeks he remained, reflecting on what had been
revealed to him, wondering if there was any possibility that the
insight he had been granted could ever be communicated. His first
thought was that he should remain in seclusion,
but the compassion for which the Buddha
became renowned dictated that he should
return to the world, to teach and devote
the rest of his life to 'Turning the Wheel
of the Law'. He walked the hundred
miles to Saranath, seeking the five men
who had deserted him. If they could be
made to understand, there was the chance

that others might be made to understand as well. He found them in the Deer Park in Saranath.

When they saw him their first response was to reject him. They were determined on a path of extreme asceticism, and they saw only what they considered to be his weakness. Even so there was something about this man that was undeniably powerful, and despite themselves they entered into a debate. Slowly they began to understand. They began to see what he had seen. Over days, not only by the power of his teaching, but also by the power of his presence, one by one, he led them to a state of Enlightenment.

From this he knew that others could also be led to understanding, and having made a spiritual journey he commenced a physical one, a journey which would last for forty-five years, during which time he wandered from place to place teaching, his brotherhood, or sangha, growing and growing, with more and more men and women coming to achieve what he had achieved. Buddhism speaks of what can be understood and known when there is a determination to go beyond the world as it is usually experienced, when there is a determination to arise out of the sleep of life and achieve what the Buddha described as Nirvana.

His Teaching

So what were the truths that the Buddha managed to convince his first five followers of in the Deer Park? At the heart of this discourse were what became known as the Four Noble Truths. These take the form of a formal medical diagnosis as to the mass of ill that is associated with life. As with all medical assessment it consists of diagnosis and treatment. Life is suffering. Suffering is caused by craving. There can be an end to suffering. There is a way that leads to the end of suffering.

The first of these Truths explores how life has about it an essential suffering, not only the obvious suffering caused by disease and death, but also the suffering caused by loss: the loss of one's loved ones, the loss of those things that one holds dear.

It pointed out that even when one is in possession of something there is the fear of loss. We strive and strain to get what we want and then fear to lose. All this involves suffering.

What the Buddha claims is that the five elements that constitute the individual all have inherent within them the element of suffering. The five elements to which he refers are the physical body, sensation and feeling, cognition, individual characteristics and consciousness.

Clearly what is being referred to here are the constituent elements which go to make this so-called individual. To the Buddha all of these are not so much a hierarchy of elements, more a series of dependencies, none of which can stand by itself alone. Every part is reliant on every other part rather than gathered round a personal identity, or soul. There is nothing left to cling to as some kind of separate self. With a conclusion of this kind the individual is forced to give way. It is in fact blown away, and this is the literal meaning of the word nirvana.

The second of the four Noble Truths identifies the source of suffering as craving. The first of these cravings is the strong desire for all that is pleasant in life, the thirst for sensual satisfaction, with the mind constantly fixed on achieving ways of gaining that satisfaction. The second craving is for life itself, the desire to cling on and possess. The third is the opposite, the desire to reject, revile and finally to destroy. This desire can at best take the form of aversion to those things that we find unpleasant, at worst to an entirely destructive attitude to life out of which arises a whole range of criticism, and general negativity. Inevitably there is something that lies at the heart of all this desire and aversion, a forceful sense of self-identification, the ego and all its conflicting demands.

The Third Noble Truth makes it quite clear that there is a cure from this mass of suffering, and that cure is the direct result of the ending of craving by renouncing it, rejecting it, by non-attachment to it. When the bond is broken, freedom arises. This is clearly a path of self-abnegation, and it is the little self, the realm of me and mine, that according to the Buddha's course of treatment needs to be dissolved. This act of dissolution is nirvana. As his was not a philosophy of attainment – in fact the attempt to try and seize something as a personal possession, does nothing, according to the Buddha, but reinforce the separate self – he would not be drawn as to what lay beyond, but the blissful expression on the face of countless images of the meditating Buddha gives an indication of what occurs when the confines of the heart and mind give way.

What are these confines? The Buddha said they were greed, hatred and delusion. When these are dissolved then the truth is revealed, love is revealed and generosity of spirit is revealed. These are not to be sought for and grasped by some imaginary individual. They naturally arise when this little self is laid down.

Within the Fourth Noble Truth is an outline of the treatment prescribed by the Buddha to bring about the end of suffering. This treatment involves the development of the following: Right View, Right Resolve, Right Speech, Right Action, Right Livelihood, Right Effort, Right Mindfulness, Right Meditation. All of this constitutes the Middle Way, the path in life in which the extremes of excessive indulgence and excessive austerity are avoided. This is the path that leads out of delusion towards the truth.

The word 'path' suggests a journey, and here are contained a series of recommended actions which will allow that journey to be made. As has already been stated, the Buddha was more interested in practice than metaphysical speculation, and what is listed here are practical measures which if employed have an utterly transformative effect. They are measures that should be adopted by those who wish to free themselves from the cycle of samsara, the cycle of life and death.

Although the Buddha taught that there is, in the final analysis, no individual identity as such, those things to which we devote ourselves have a karmic effect on future lives which arise 'like one fire lit from another'.

When looking at the Eightfold Path it becomes evident that the eight may be divided into three distinct areas of life, areas that were of particular concern to the Buddha. These are wisdom, morality and meditation.

Wisdom involves Right View or coming to a proper understanding of the truth of the Buddha's teaching. All of us have had an insight, a flash of understanding, when our view suddenly changes. With that flash arises the realization that life as we know it has its limitations. In moments of greater awareness the sense of separation normally experienced gives way to a deep appreciation of the underlying unity, a unity from which we are in no way separate. From this experience there may arise a resolution to come to a deeper and more lasting understanding of the true nature of things. This is Right Resolve, and as part of this resolution there may arise the steady determination to meet and counter those deep ingrained habits of heart and mind that force us into a state of separation and suffering. Involving both heart and mind, the decision to be made is both emotional and intellectual. This is the second aspect of wisdom.

Morality involves speech, action and the way we gain our livelihood. Right Speech concerns the truth, holding the words of truth in mind, and speaking from that truth in a way that is true. This doesn't mean that these words remain as a set of ideas but are the words of truth discovered in experience and spoken in a way that causes no harm.

Words are all important. Our experience of the world is forged out of the ideas that we carry with us. If we avoid not only lying to others but also lying to ourselves, everything will not only be freed from the distortions we have imposed but will become purified and therefore more translucent and luminous.

Right Action is a direct result of refined ideas. If our words are of the nature of greed, hatred and delusion then must our action be likewise. How different are actions that arise out of their opposites: generosity, compassion and understanding. These are skilful actions which are quite different from the clumsy results of egotistical prompting. Actions such as these, because of the limits placed upon them by the nature of their source, are bound to be mistimed and mis-measured, and rather than unify and resolve, will inevitably create division. Skilful actions, which draw together and break down division, come from an altogether different source and have an altogether different quality.

Right Livelihood encourages us to seek a way of sustaining ourselves which minimizes the impact we have on others and the world. In gaining our living we may feel that circumstances force us into ignoring such considerations, but Right Livelihood encourages us to think differently, to appreciate the interconnectedness of all things and to tread lightly with care.

The third main area dealt with in the Eightfold Path is meditation. This is not surprising given that Siddhartha became the Buddha through single pointed meditation. He resolved to attain Enlightenment. He sat upon the ground and swore that 'Flesh may wither, blood may dry up, but I shall not leave this seat until I gain Enlightenment!' Such resolution is therefore an essential part of the meditative process, to remain undeflected and undeterred regardless of the difficulties encountered. Inevitably there are mental traits, deep ingrained habits of heart and mind which need to be countered with steady determination.

Right Mindfulness is one of the great joys of the reflective life. When we adopt mindfulness we immediately allow for quiet observation; the possibility that, rather than being utterly identified with all the thoughts and feelings which rise in the heart and mind, we have the capacity to stand back and quietly observe the promptings of self-identification. What Mindfulness also does is draw us out of all the concerns for the past and future, all the confusion that arises out of a self-created imaginary world, and to bring us back to the immediate reality of the here and now. To be dominated by thoughts and feelings which are in a state of constant flux is not a way of bringing steadiness and

consistency to our actions. The movements of the mind are many; the unidentified observer is unitary, therefore, calm and clear.

Calmness and clarity are much desired, but personal desire will never provide them. Desire has the opposite effect. It agitates rather than calms. It confuses rather than clarifies. But as has already been stated, quiet determination is another thing. It involves laying aside all wishes for oneself, giving up this little self and recognising it for what it is, a matrix of elements. It is not therefore some kind of personal attainment that is being sought in meditation, but rather a dissolution of all that holds us confined. Remember the Buddha's own experience watching his father ploughing whilst he sat in the shade of a rose-apple tree, of how he quite naturally slipped below the surface of life and discovered 'Enlightenment'. It is about dissolving and merging, the key ingredients of the reflective life. And it is reflection that is being offered by this book, words to be carried into daily life, to be held in mind as an oasis of peace and bliss.

Although the daily reflections which follow are drawn primarily from the Pali Texts which formed the original corpus of Buddhist thinking, even those that are not are much respected and therefore in accord with the Buddha's original teaching. The very fact that the texts have been chosen for reflection is very much in keeping with the Buddha's avowed purpose, not speculation but transformation. As has already been stressed, Buddhism is a practical philosophy. These texts are for a practical purpose.

To reflect upon the words of the Buddha, to allow them to suffuse the heart and mind is a time-honoured way of coming to a true understanding of what is meant. This is not theoretical understanding – yet more ideas to add to the general stock of information we already possess. Reflecting upon these texts will allow there to arise a deeper understanding of how to live in harmony and not discord, in unity and not division, in Truth and not delusion.

Carry the book with you or write down the day's thought for continual reference. Many of these texts were learnt by heart and passed on from generation to generation. Why not follow suit and learn some of them by heart, especially those that have a particular resonance? Rather than making up your mind as to their meaning, hold them in mind and allow their significance to have its effect on the way you experience life.

Reflections

May all be happy
and at their ease!
May they be joyous and
live in safety!

So I went forth from home in
the houseless state, a quester
of what is good, seeking the
incomparable path to peace.

Standing or walking,
sitting or lying down,
during all these waking hours,
let him establish mindfulness of good
will, which men call the highest state!

'When you spoke of
wholesome dharmas which
ones did you mean?'
'I meant morality,
faith, vigour, mindfulness
and concentration.'

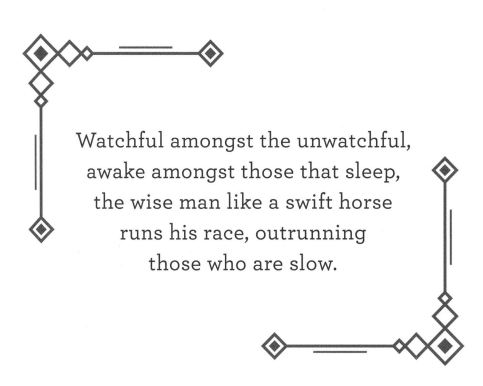

Watchful amongst the unwatchful,
awake amongst those that sleep,
the wise man like a swift horse
runs his race, outrunning
those who are slow.

What we are today comes
from our thoughts of yesterday,
and present thoughts build
our life of tomorrow:
our life is the creation of our mind.

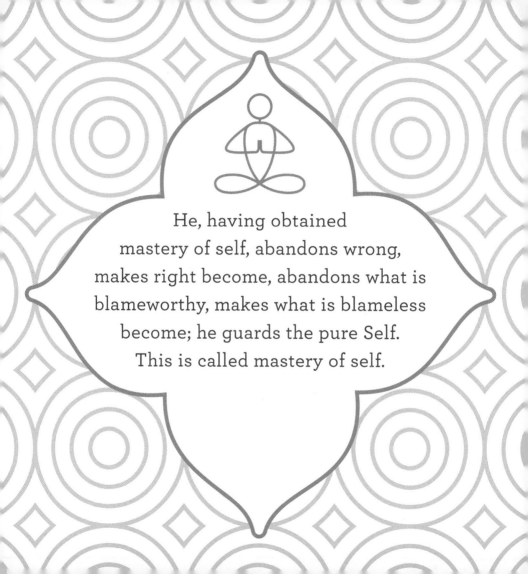

He, having obtained
mastery of self, abandons wrong,
makes right become, abandons what is
blameworthy, makes what is blameless
become; he guards the pure Self.
This is called mastery of self.

Gautama lives as one who has
laid aside the club and sword.
He is scrupulous, kindly, friendly and
compassionate towards all breathing things.

As a builder of a city when constructing a town first of all clears the site, removes all stumps and thorns, and levels it; and only after that he lays out and marks off the roads and cross-roads, and so builds the city, even so the Yogin develops the five cardinal virtues with morality as his support, with morality as his basis.

If a man speaks or acts with an impure mind,
suffering follows him as the wheel of the cart
follows the beast that draws it.

He who for the sake of happiness hurts others who also want happiness, shall not hereafter find happiness.

When faith arises it arrests
the Five Hindrances and the heart becomes free
from them, clear, serene and undisturbed.

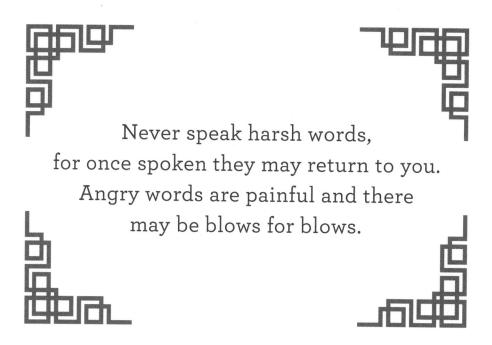

Never speak harsh words,
for once spoken they may return to you.
Angry words are painful and there
may be blows for blows.

To neglect the highest
dharma, and instead to
think demeritorious thoughts,
is like neglecting the jewels on
the jewel-island and collecting
lumps of earth instead.

Abandoning what is unwholesome, you ought to ponder what is wholesome, for that will bring you advantages in this world and help you to win the highest goal.

When the recluse
speaks much,
'tis of and on the goal;
knowing of dharma
tells, knowing he
speaketh much.

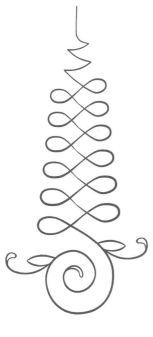

When wisdom arises it dispels
the darkness of ignorance,
generates the illumination
of knowledge, sheds the light
of cognition and makes holy
truths stand out clearly.

If material shape is impermanent,
and if that which impermanent is suffering,
you cannot regard that which is impermanent,
suffering and liable to change as:
This is mine, I am this, this is my Self.

The wise do not take delight in
the senses and their objects,
are not impressed by them,
are not attached to them and
in consequence their craving ceases.

If a man speaks or
acts with a pure mind,
joy follows him
as his own shadow.

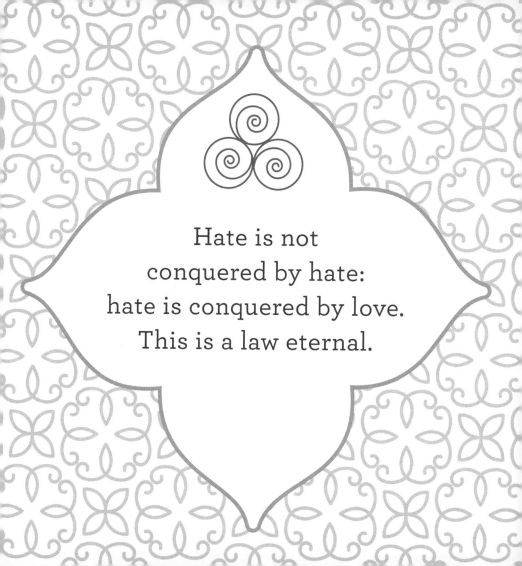

Hate is not
conquered by hate:
hate is conquered by love.
This is a law eternal.

This contemplation is one which I, mindful, enter upon and mindful emerge from.

The cessation of craving
successively leads to that of grasping,
of becoming, of birth,
of old age and death,
of grief, lamentation, pain,
sadness and despair.

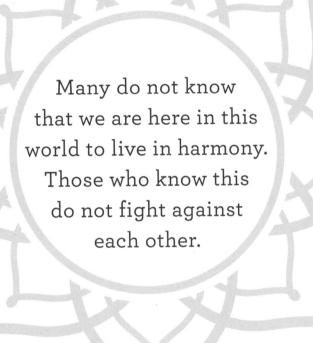

Many do not know
that we are here in this
world to live in harmony.
Those who know this
do not fight against
each other.

As a mountain
peak is free from
all desire to please
or displease,
so is nirvana.

As the lotus is unstained by water,
so is nirvana unstained
by the defilements.

Who passion and hate and ignorance
have left, him they call one who
has made the self become,
who is Brahma-become,
truth finder, an awakened one,
who's passed by fear and dread,
one who has abandoned
everything.

For whatever a man thinks about continually, to that his mind becomes inclined by force of habit.

The sense pleasures are
not worth paying any attention to,
for they are unreal, hollow, and uncertain,
and the happiness they give
is merely imaginary.

Warded in act and word,
in eating temperate,
with truth I clear the weeds;
and full of bliss is my deliverance.

Men who are foolish and ignorant are
careless and never watchful;
but the man who lives in watchfulness
considers it his greatest treasure.

This dharma I teach is deep,
difficult to see, difficult to understand,
peaceful, excellent, beyond dialectic,
subtle, intelligible to the wise.

As cool water allays feverish heat,
so also nirvana removes the craving
for sensuous enjoyments,
the craving for further becoming,
the cessation of becoming.

The royal chariots
wear out,
and so too
the body ages.
The true dharma
does not age.

Never surrender to carelessness;
never sink into weak pleasures
and lust. Those who are watchful,
in deep contemplation, reach
the end, the joy supreme.

A brightly shining fire,
when not stirred by the
wind, is soon appeased;
so the unstimulated
heart of those who live
in seclusion wins peace
without much effort.

Hidden in the mystery of consciousness, the mind, incorporeal, flies alone far away. Those who set their mind on harmony become free from the bonds of death.

A person who is neither tempter of self nor a
tormentor of others is, in this very life,
stilled, attained to nirvana, become cool;
he is one who experiences bliss; he lives with
a self that has become Brahma.

An enemy can hurt an enemy,
and a man who hates can harm another
man; but a man's own mind, if wrongly
directed, can do him a far
greater harm.

Loss of mindfulness
is why people engage in
useless pursuits, do not
care for their own interests
and remain unalarmed in
the presence of things which
actually menace
their welfare.

By the All-awakened One,
foreknowing, thoroughly
knowing every world,
opened is the door of
the deathless;
when nirvana has
been reached
there is security.

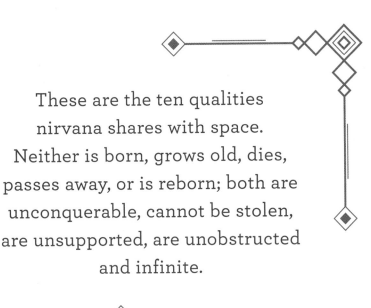

These are the ten qualities
nirvana shares with space.
Neither is born, grows old, dies,
passes away, or is reborn; both are
unconquerable, cannot be stolen,
are unsupported, are unobstructed
and infinite.

As a mountain peak is inaccessible, so is nirvana inaccessible to all passions. As no seed can grow on a mountain peak, so the seeds of all the passions cannot grow in nirvana.

The mind is wavering and restless,
difficult to guard and restrain.
Let the wise man straighten his mind
as a maker of arrows makes
his arrow straight.

A mind which is not protected by mindfulness is as helpless as a blind man walking over uneven ground without a guide.

As the bee takes the essence of
a flower and flies away without
destroying its beauty and perfume,
so let the sage wander in this life.

The holy disciple who has followed the
right road sees nirvana with a mind which
is pure, sublime, straight, unimpeded and
disinterested.

In whom no craving spreads,
in the monk who cuts the stream,
rid of all toils and tasks,
no fret is found or known.

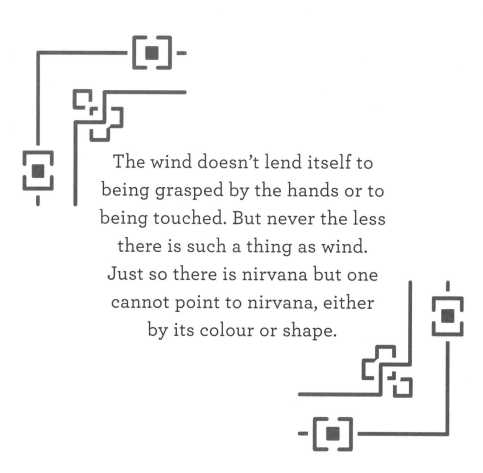

The wind doesn't lend itself to
being grasped by the hands or to
being touched. But never the less
there is such a thing as wind.
Just so there is nirvana but one
cannot point to nirvana, either
by its colour or shape.

For those following
the stream of becoming,
who are overcome by touches?
Proceeding by the false way,
distant is the destruction
of the fetters.

Him the unprovokable, him the unclouded
mind, freed of all lustfulness, void of all indolence,
guide of those on the brink, is master of
birth-and-death.

'These are my sons.
This is my wealth.'
In this way the fool troubles
himself. He is not the
owner of himself:
how much less of his sons
and his wealth!

The man plunges in the spate,
flooding and turgid swift of flow,
he, borne along the current's way,
how can he others help to cross?

People are tied down by a sense object
when they cover it with unreal imaginations;
likewise they are liberated when they
see it as it really is.

The wrong action seems sweet
to the fool until the reaction comes and brings
pain, and the bitter fruits of wrong deeds have then
to be eaten by the fool.

Arise (from sloth), sir (meditating);
train swiftly for tranquility.
Let not death's king find you proud,
nor dupe you to subjection.

Slothfulness is dust...
Being prone to it is dust:
by diligence, by knowledge,
draw out the barb of self.

And if to his own harm the fool increases in cleverness, this only destroys his own mind, and his fate is worse than before.

Spotless, unobstructed, silent,
like the vast expanse of space;
who in truth does really see Thee?
The Tathagata perceives.

Faith is the seed,
austerity the rain,
wisdom my yoke and plough;
my pole is modesty;
my mind is the strap
and I have mindfulness
for share and goad.

Look upon the man who tells thee thy faults as if he told thee of hidden treasure, the wise man who shows thee the dangers of life. Follow that man: he who follows him will see good and not evil.

Not from anywhere
Thou comest, and to
nowhere dost thou go;
in no dwelling place
have the sages
ever apprehended
Thee.

Who here in faith, in
moral habit grows,
in wisdom, in giving up and in the heard,
such as she, a disciple of moral habit,
here wins what is the
essence of the self.

Not through what is low comes the
attainment of the highest,
but through what is high comes
the attainment of the highest.

Have not for friends those
whose soul is ugly; go not
with men who have an evil soul.
Have for friends those whose
soul is beautiful; go with
men whose soul is good.

If your sense-organs are calm,
so will the acts of the body become calm,
calm the acts of speech,
calm the acts of mind; and one
may think: 'We will offer an
offering – calm itself – to our
fellow Brahma-farers.'

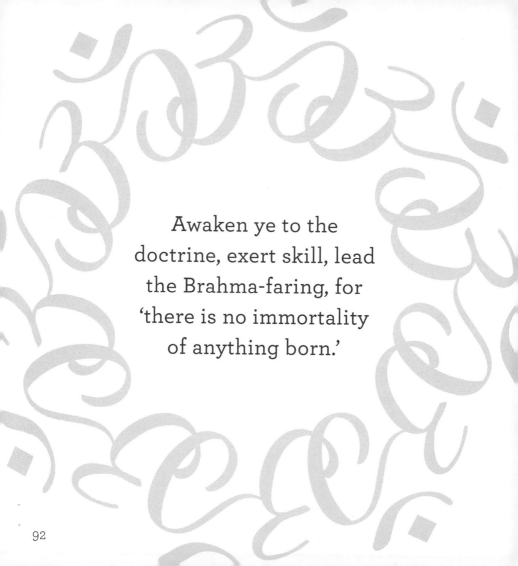

Awaken ye to the doctrine, exert skill, lead the Brahma-faring, for 'there is no immortality of anything born.'

In whatever person malice is engendered,
in that person love should be made
to become, also compassion,
also balance.

Learn this from the river's flow
in mountain cleft and chasm:
loud gush the rivulets,
the great stream silent moves.
Loud booms the empty thing.
The full is ever calm;
like pot half-full the fool,
like full pot the sage.

Who knows and
curbed-of-self, tho' knowing,
speaks not much:
the sage and wisdom
worths, that sage still
wisdom wins.

Just as a flower which seems beautiful
and has colour but has no perfume,
so are the fruitless words
of the man who speaks them
but does them not.

As all plants and animals which increase
and grow and prosper, do so with the earth
as their support, with the earth as their basis,
just so the Yogin, with morality as his support,
with morality as his basis, develops the
five cardinal virtues:
faith, vigour, mindfulness,
concentration and wisdom.

When invaded by painful
feeling, the Arahat firmly
grasps at the idea of
impermanence, and ties
his thoughts to the post
of contemplation.

Death carries away the man who gathers
the flowers of sensuous passions, even as
a torrent of rushing waters overflows a
sleeping village, and then runs forward
on its way.

From the utter fading away
and stopping of ignorance the constructions
stop, and so stops each of the rest. Such is
the stopping of this entire mass of ill.

Joy is born in one who has delight,
the body of one who has joy is calmed,
one whose body is calmed feels ease,
and the mind of one who is at ease
is contemplative.

Wherefore stir up energy for the
attainment of the unattained,
for the mastery of the unmastered,
for the realization of the unrealized.
Thus will your going forth
become a barren but fruitful
and growing thing.

Make the Self
your refuge
and your lamp.

Secluded meditation guards him who meditates, lengthens his life, gives him strength and shuts out faults.

To what end should the thought:
'I am the result of my own deeds,
heir to deeds, having deeds
for matrix, deeds for kin;
to me the deeds come
home again;
whatever deed I do,
whether good or evil,
I shall become its heir,'
be contemplated often
by man or woman?

Overcome anger by peacefulness: overcome evil by good. Overcome the mean by generosity; and the man who lies by truth.

The Brahma-faring is lived for the advantage of
the training, for the further wisdom, for the
essence of freedom, for mastery in mindfulness.

Those who are forever watchful,
who study themselves day and night,
and who wholly strive for nirvana,
all their passions pass away.

The Great Way is calm
and large hearted,
for it nothing is easy,
nothing hard.

Those who have high thoughts are ever striving:
they are not happy to remain in the same place.
Like swans that leave their lake and rise into the
air, they leave their home for a higher home.

Small views
are irresolute,
the more in haste,
the tardier
they go.

The man who controls his senses as a good driver controls his horses, and who is free from lower passions and pride, is admired even by the gods.

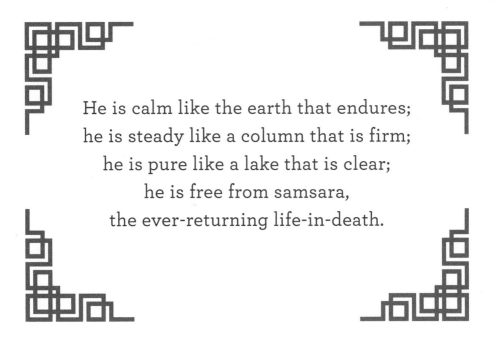

He is calm like the earth that endures;
he is steady like a column that is firm;
he is pure like a lake that is clear;
he is free from samsara,
the ever-returning life-in-death.

Better than a thousand useless words is one word that gives peace.

Obey the nature of things,
and you are in concord with
The Way, calm and easy and
free from annoyance.

In the light of his vision he has
found his freedom:
his thoughts are peace and
his work is peace.

When Mind and each
believing mind are not divided,
and undivided are each
believing mind and Mind,
this is where words fail;
for it is not of the past,
present or future.

If a man should conquer in battle
a thousand and thousand more,
and another should conquer himself,
his would be the greater victory,
because the greatest of victories is
the victory over oneself.

Stopping of
becoming
is nirvana.

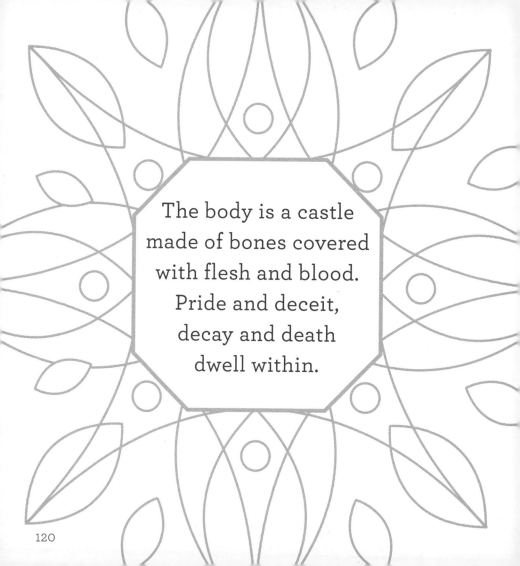

The body is a castle
made of bones covered
with flesh and blood.
Pride and deceit,
decay and death
dwell within.

Whoever should intentionally deprive a breathing thing of life, there is an offence of expiation.

'He insulted me, he hurt me,
he defeated me, he robbed me.'
Those who think such things
will not be free from hate.

Pursue not the outer entanglements,
dwell not on the Inner Void;
be serene in the oneness of things,
and dualism vanishes by itself.

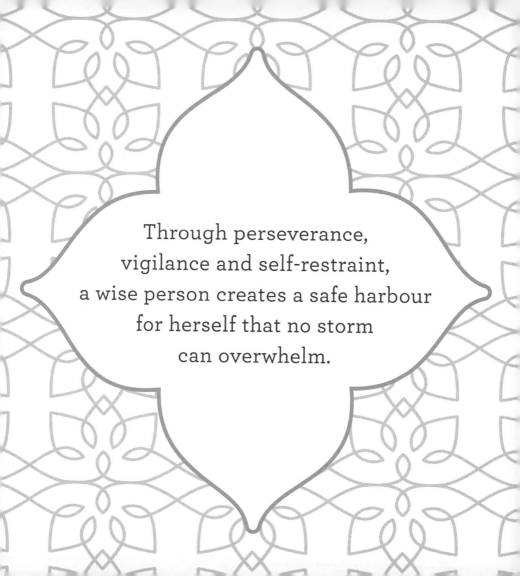

Through perseverance,
vigilance and self-restraint,
a wise person creates a safe harbour
for herself that no storm
can overwhelm.

As from a large heap of flowers many
garlands and wreaths are made, so
by a mortal in this
life there is much good
work to be done.

The wise one does not judge others, not their words or deeds or what they have or have not done. The wise one only contemplates her own words and deeds.

How long is the night to the watchman; how long is the road to the weary; how long is the wandering of lives ending in death for the fool who cannot find the path!

When we return to the root,
we gain the meaning; when we
pursue external objects we
lose the reason.

Those who think the unreal is,
and the Real is not,
they shall never reach the
Truth, lost in the path
of wrong thought.

If an eye never falls asleep,
all dreams will by themselves cease.

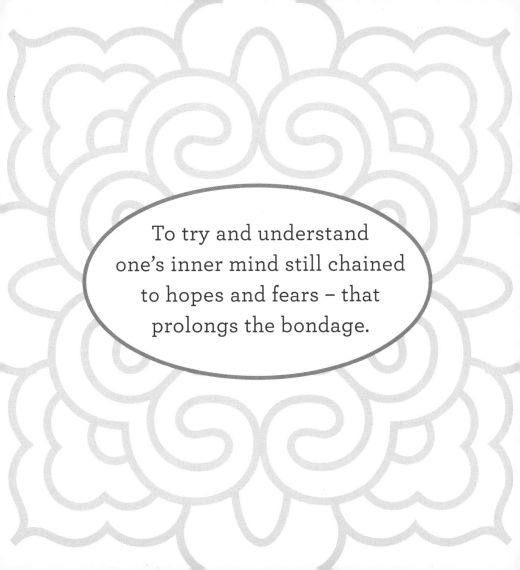

To try and understand
one's inner mind still chained
to hopes and fears – that
prolongs the bondage.

Who makes unbounded
love to become,
mindful, he sees the
attachments all destroyed.

If during the whole of life a fool
lives with a wise man, he never
knows the path of wisdom as
the spoon never knows the
taste of soup.

Deeds done in harmony
with one's path of life are
those which bring
clarity and peace and
harmony to the doer.

Those who make channels for water control the water; makers of arrows make the arrows straight; carpenters control their timber; and the wise control their own minds.

In whatever person malice is engendered, in that person love should be made to become, also compassion, also balance.

Whoever offers sacrifice,
or whoever gets others to do so –
all these are following a course of
merit benefiting many others.

Whosoever honours in reverence those
who are old in virtue and holiness,
he indeed conquers four treasures:
long life and health, and power and joy.

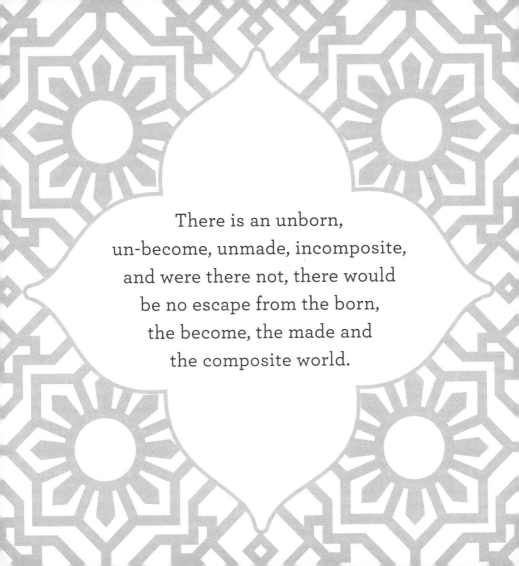

There is an unborn,
un-become, unmade, incomposite,
and were there not, there would
be no escape from the born,
the become, the made and
the composite world.

Better than a hundred years
lived in ignorance, without contemplation,
is one single day of life lived in wisdom
and deep contemplation.

Better than a hundred years lived
in idleness and in weakness is a single
day of life lived with courage and
powerful striving.

Watchfulness is the path of immortality: unwatchfulness is the path of death. Those who are watchful never die: those who do not watch are already dead.

The fool who does evil to a man
who is good, to a man who is pure
and free from sin, the evil returns
to him like dust thrown
against the wind.

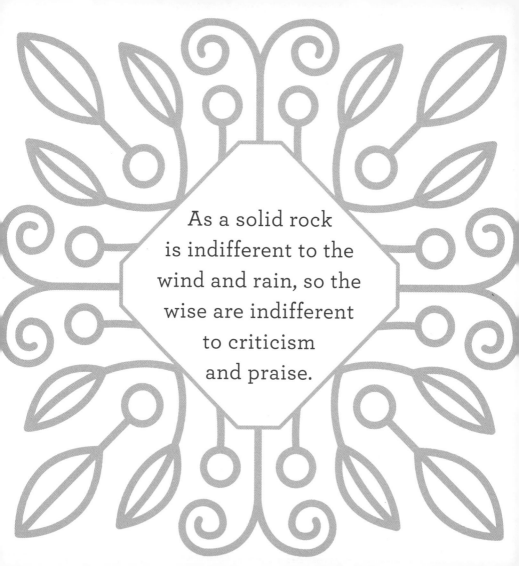

As a solid rock
is indifferent to the
wind and rain, so the
wise are indifferent
to criticism
and praise.

A man may find pleasure in evil as long
as his evil has not given fruit; but when the
fruit of evil comes then that man finds
evil indeed.

Abandon the ways of confusion and darkness and live in the light of peace and harmony.

Have fire like a noble horse
touched by the whip.
By faith, by virtue,
by wisdom and by right
action, you shall overcome
the sorrows of life.

The moment we
are enlightened within,
we go beyond the
voidness of a world
confronting us.

Hold not a sin of little worth,
thinking 'this is little to me'.
The falling of drops of water
will in time fill a water-jar.
Even so the foolish man
becomes full of evil although
he gather it little by little.

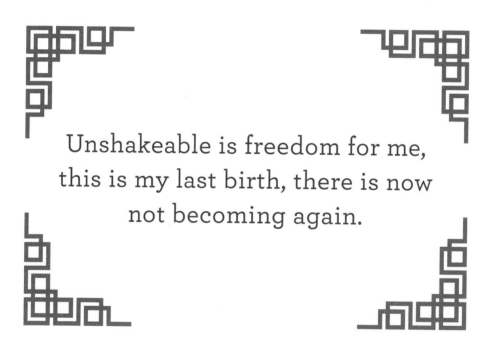

Unshakeable is freedom for me,
this is my last birth, there is now
not becoming again.

All beings fear before danger,
life is dear to all. When a man
considers this, he does not kill or
cause to kill.

Stirred up for me shall unsluggish energy
become, called up unmuddled mindfulness;
calm and serene my body, not turbulent;
concentrated my mind and one-pointed.

I have gone round in vain
the cycles of many lives, ever striving to find the
builder of the house of life that must die! But now
I have seen thee, house builder: never more shalt
thou build this house. The rafters of sin are broken,
the ridge-pole of ignorance is destroyed. The fever
of craving is past: for my mortal mind is gone to
the joy of nirvana.

To aim at lasting achievements
whilst still exposed to this
world's distractions – that prolongs
the bondage.

So impermanent are the
constructions, so transient,
so unreliable.

If a man tries not to learn
he grows old just like an ox!
His body indeed grows old,
but his wisdom does not grow.

Anyone in whom
passion is abandoned,
in whom delusion
is abandoned,
is called one not
bound by death.

O let us live in joy,
in love amongst those
who hate!
Among men who hate,
let us live in love.

Who passion for all pleasure ends, helped by
the state of man-of-naught, rid of all else, is
yondermost release of all sense released,
he would stay poised untrammelled
in that state.

Not to be helpful to others,
not to give to those in need,
this is the fruit of samsara.
Better than this is to renounce
the idea of self.

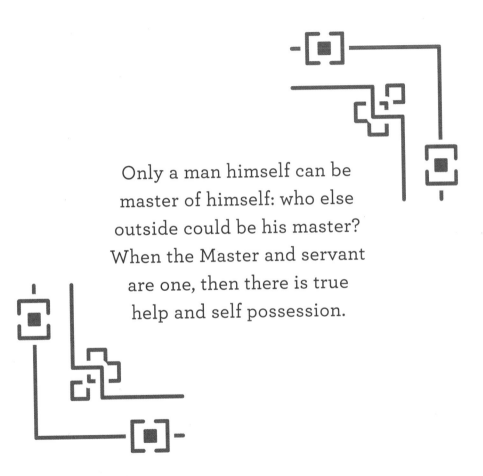

Only a man himself can be
master of himself: who else
outside could be his master?
When the Master and servant
are one, then there is true
help and self possession.

Any wrong or evil a man
does is born in himself and is
caused by himself; and this crushes
the foolish man as a hard stone
grinds the weaker stone.

If one find a friend with whom to fare,
rapt in the well-abiding apt,
surmounting dangers one and all
with joy fare with him mindfully.

O let us live in joy,
in peace amongst those
who struggle!
Among men who struggle,
let us live in peace.

If you can be in silent quietness like a broken gong that is silent, you have reached the peace of nirvana and your anger is peace.

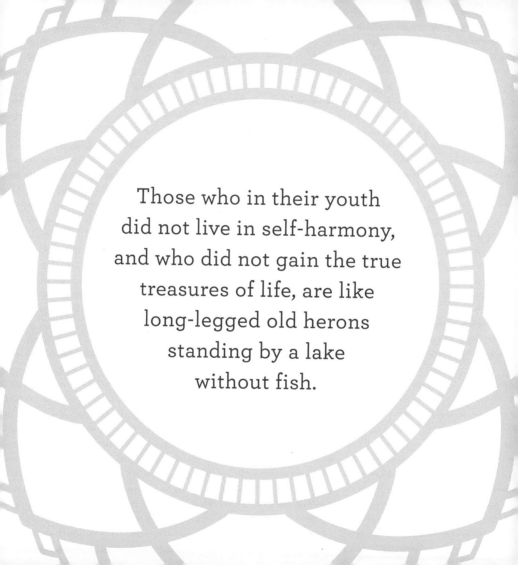

Those who in their youth
did not live in self-harmony,
and who did not gain the true
treasures of life, are like
long-legged old herons
standing by a lake
without fish.

Through stillness joined to insight true, his passions are annihilated. Stillness must first of all be found, that springs from disregarding worldly satisfactions.

Form should be seen as a mass of
foam, because easily crushed;
feeling as a water bubble,
because pleasurable only for a
moment; perception as a
mirage, because delusive.

The presence always of Mara,
the Lord of Death – do you understand
that? Even the rich man when he is laid low,
departs alone – do you understand that?

With passion gone and hate expelled,
let him in boundless measure then quicken
a heart of love, every day and night zeal
suffuse all quarters to infinitude.

Even as a great rock
is not shaken by
the wind, the wise
man is not shaken
by praise or blame.

He who for himself or others
craves not for sons or power or
wealth, who puts not his own success
before the success of righteousness,
he is virtuous, and righteous
and wise.

If a man does something wrong,
let him not do it again and again.
Let him find no pleasure in his sin.
Painful is the accumulation
of wrongdoings.

If a man do something good,
let him do it again and again.
Let him find joy in his good work.
Joyful is the accumulation of
good work.

A man may find pain in doing
good as long as his good has not given
fruit; but when the fruit of good comes
then that man finds good indeed.

Then you forfeit the truth of the real; your fallen condition shocks you no longer. Burning with grief you yearn for re-union with him whom you cherish.

Palaces built of earth and stone and
wood, wealthy men endowed with food and
dress and finery, legions of retainers who
throng round the mighty – these are like castles
in the air, like rainbows in the sky, and how
deluded those who think of this as truth.

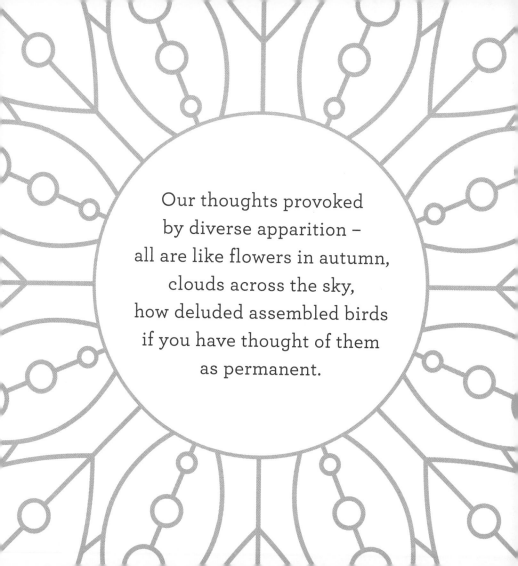

Our thoughts provoked
by diverse apparition –
all are like flowers in autumn,
clouds across the sky,
how deluded assembled birds
if you have thought of them
as permanent.

For he whose mind is well trained in the ways
that lead to light, who surrenders the bondage
of attachments and finds joy in his freedom
from bondage, who free from the darkness
of passions shines pure in radiance of light,
even in this mortal life, he enjoys the
immortal nirvana.

He who is pleasure-quit, as
conqueror fares,
hath found and known the end
of birth-and-death.
Cool man, cool as the waters
of the lake.

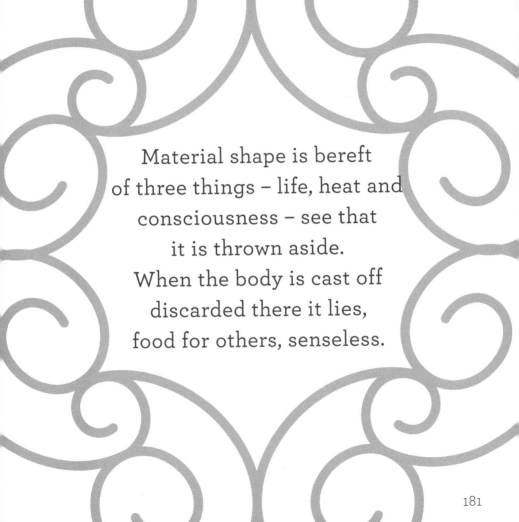

Material shape is bereft
of three things – life, heat and
consciousness – see that
it is thrown aside.
When the body is cast off
discarded there it lies,
food for others, senseless.

Make haste and do
what is good; keep your
mind away from evil.
If a man is slow in doing
good, his mind finds
pleasure in evil.

And so he dwells recognizing
himself in all, suffusing the entire world
with a heart linked to friendliness, far-
reaching, wide-spread, free, unlimited, free
from enmity and malice.

One who values happiness
for himself but creates anxiety
for others is confused.

The man
who has no evil
cannot be hurt
by evil.

Dharma is truth,
restraint is Brahma-faring,
The Middle Way pursuing,
brahman, the way to Brahma-attainment.
Due honour pay thou to the
upright-minded,
who so doth this, him do
I call Tide-rider.

Even as rain breaks through
an ill-thatched house,
passions will break through
an ill-guarded mind.

Gone greed, gone guile,
gone thirst, gone grudge,
and winnowed all
delusions, faults,
wantless in all the
world become.

Good friends at one time,
of a sudden they dislike you.
You try to please them,
quite in vain – the worldly are
not easily contented.

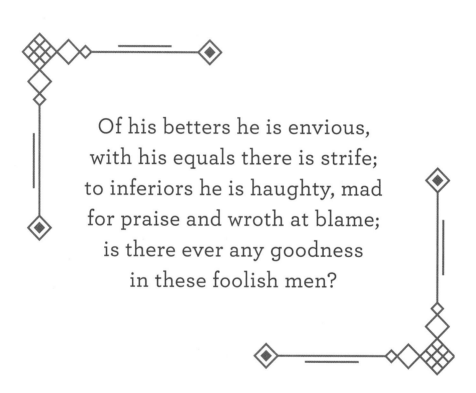

Of his betters he is envious,
with his equals there is strife;
to inferiors he is haughty, mad
for praise and wroth at blame;
is there ever any goodness
in these foolish men?

He who lives only for pleasures, and whose soul is not in harmony, who considers not the food he eats, is idle and has not the power of virtue – such a man is moved by Mara, is moved by selfish temptations, even as a weak tree is shaken by the wind.

Let him be strenuous, upright and truly straight,
without conceit of self, easily contented and joyous,
free of cares; let him not be submerged by things
of this world; let him not take upon the burden of
worldly goods; let his senses be controlled; let him
be wise, not puffed up and let him not desire great
possessions even for his family. Let him do nothing
that is mean or that the wise would reprove.

Self-applause, belittling others,
or encouragement to sin,
some such evil's sure to happen where
one fool meets another.

The fools are no one's friends, so have
the Buddhas taught us;
they cannot love unless their interest
in themselves impels them.

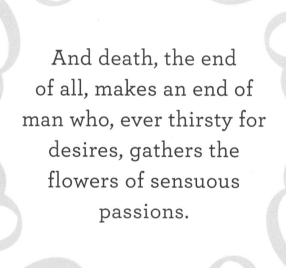

And death, the end
of all, makes an end of
man who, ever thirsty for
desires, gathers the
flowers of sensuous
passions.

Consciousness
is unending.

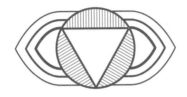

Think not of the faults of others,
of what they have done or not done.
Think rather of your own sins,
of the things you have done
or not done.

He hears dharma and learns it by heart, examines the import of things so learnt and is in an ecstasy of delight over them; strong desire rises in him; he is emboldened; he weighs it all; he strives; being self-resolute, by means of body, he realizes the highest truth itself.

Who, unless he be quite mad,
would make plans which do reckon
with death, when he sees the world so
unsubstantial and frail, like a water bubble?

Even as on a heap of rubbish thrown away by the side of the road, a lotus flower may grow and blossom with its pure perfume giving joy to the soul, in the same way among the blind multitudes shines pure the light of wisdom of the student who follows the Buddha, the One who is truly awake.

What is clinging? There are four kinds of clinging: Clinging to pleasure. Clinging to views. Clinging to rules, techniques and vows. Clinging to self.

And from all other cares released, the mind set on collecting my own spirit, to unify and discipline my spirit I will strive.

Invisible and subtle
is the mind, and it flies after
fancies wherever it likes:
but let the wise man guard
well his mind, for a mind
well guarded is a source
of great joy.

Neither in the sky,
nor in the deep in the ocean,
nor in a mountain-cave,
nor anywhere, can a man be
free from the evil he
has done.

A man who has imposed strict mindfulness
on all he does, and remains as watchful as a
gatekeeper at a city-gate, is safe from injury
by the passions, just as a well guarded town is
safe from its foes.

The instructed disciple disregards material shapes and the rest; by disregarding he is passionless; through passionlessness he is freed; in freedom, the knowledge comes to be – I am freed – and he has foreknowledge: Destroyed is birth, lived is the Brahma-faring, done is what was done, there is nothing more of being such or such.

Grasping after systems,
imprisoned by dogmas for the most part is this
world. But he who does not go in for system-
grasping he neither doubts nor is perplexed;
by not depending on others, knowledge herein
comes to be his own.

Train yourself in
this way: from higher
to higher, from strength
to strength we will
strive, and we will come
to realize unsurpassed
freedom.

A wrong action may not bring its reaction at once, even as fresh milk turns not sour at once: like a smoldering fire concealed under ashes it consumes the wrongdoer, the fool.

He who in early days was unwise but later found wisdom, he sheds light over the world like that of the moon when free from clouds.

I am the result of my own deeds, heir to deeds.
Whatever deed I do, whether good or evil, I shall
become its heir. This should be
contemplated often.

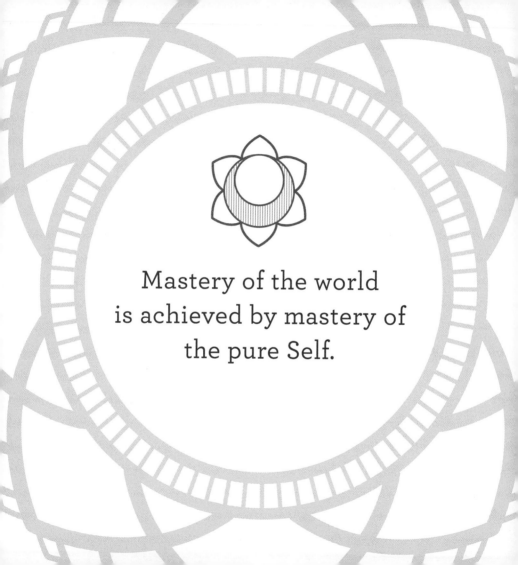

Mastery of the world
is achieved by mastery of
the pure Self.

By what earthly path could you entice
the Buddha who, enjoying all, can wander
through the pathless ways of the Infinite –
the Buddha who is awake, whose victory
cannot be turned into defeat, and whom
no one can conquer?

Stirred for me shall be unsluggish energy,
called up unmuddled mindfulness;
calmed and serene my body, not turbulent;
concentrated my mind and one-pointed.

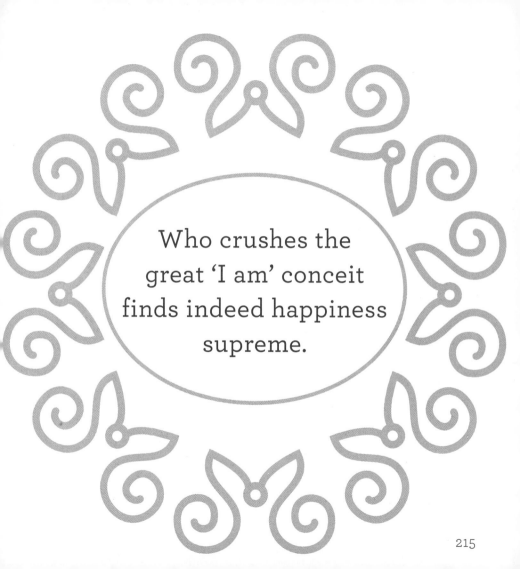

Who crushes the great 'I am' conceit finds indeed happiness supreme.

Abandon what is wrong.
It is possible to abandon it. Were it not possible
to abandon what is wrong, I would not say:
Abandon it. But because it is possible, therefore
I say: Abandon what is wrong.

Live not a low life;
remember and forget not;
follow not wrong ideas;
sink not into the world.

Swan follow the path
of the sun by the miracle
of flying through air.
Men who are strong
conquer evil and its armies;
and then rise far above
the world.

Sense pleasures are impermanent. The search for them involves suffering, and they are enjoyed in constant disquiet; their loss leads to much grief, and their gain can never result in lasting satisfaction.

Abandoning what is unwholesome, you ought to ponder what is wholesome, for that will bring you advantages in this world and help you to win the heighest goal.

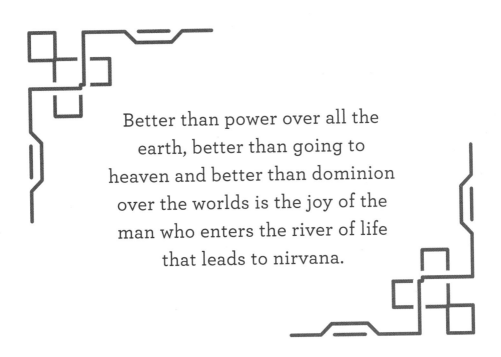

Better than power over all the earth, better than going to heaven and better than dominion over the worlds is the joy of the man who enters the river of life that leads to nirvana.

Brahma-faring is lived for
the goal of restraint,
for the goal of abandoning,
for the goal of dispassion,
for the goal of
making to cease.

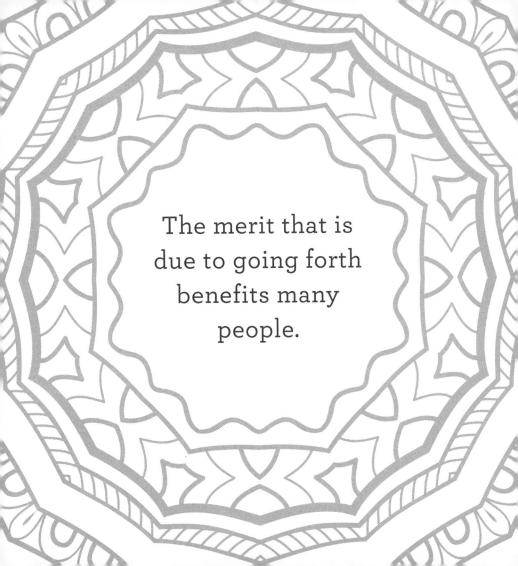

The merit that is
due to going forth
benefits many
people.

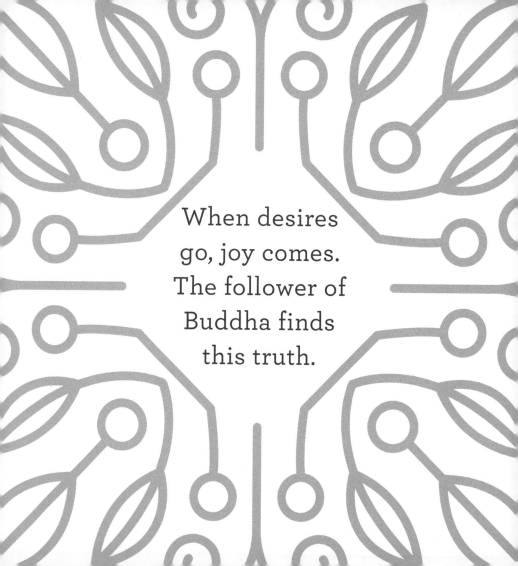

When desires
go, joy comes.
The follower of
Buddha finds
this truth.

Drench, pervade, fill and pervade this body itself with zest and ease that are born of contemplation.

Not to hurt by deeds of words,
self-control as taught in the Rules, moderation in
food, the solitude of one's room and one's bed, and
the practice of the highest consciousness: this is
the teachings of the Buddhas who are awake.

If ill-will or the desire to hurt others should stir your mind, purify it with the opposite. Friendliness and compassion are their antidotes; for they are as ever as opposed to hatred as light to darkness.

Victory brings hate, because the defeated
man is unhappy.
He who surrenders victory and defeat,
this man finds joy.

A man whose words
are lies, who transgresses the
Great Law, and who scorns
the higher world – there is
no evil this man may
not do.

The fair tree of thought that
knows no duality,
spreads through the triple world.
It bears the flower and fruit
of compassion, and its name is service
of others.

It is better to spend one day contemplating
the birth and death of all things than
a hundred years never contemplating
beginnings and endings.

He who has no craving desires,
either for this world or for another world,
who free from desires is
in infinite freedom – him
call I a Brahmin.

By oneself the evil is done
and it is oneself that suffers:
by oneself the evil is not done,
and by one's Self one
becomes pure.

He who does what should
not be done, who forgets the
true aim of life and sinks
into transient pleasures –
he will one day envy the
man who lives in
high contemplation.

'This is myself and this is another.'
Be free of this bond which encompasses
you about, and your own self is
thereby released.

From passion arises sorrow and from
passion arises fear. If a man is free from
passion, he is free from fear
and sorrow.

He who goes for refuge
to Buddha, to Truth and
to those whom he taught,
he goes indeed to a great
refuge. Then he sees the
four great truths.

Do not err in this
matter of self and other.
Everything is Buddha
without exception.
Here is that immaculate
final stage, where thought
is pure in its
true nature.

Neither him given to laxity,
nor him of little strength,
may reach nirvana,
the freedom of all ill.

There are four kinds of grasping:
grasping after sense-pleasures,
grasping after opinion, grasping after rule
and rite, grasping after the theory of 'self'.

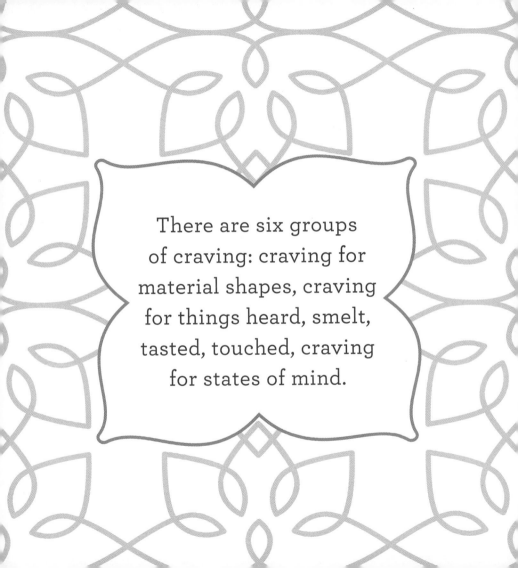

There are six groups
of craving: craving for
material shapes, craving
for things heard, smelt,
tasted, touched, craving
for states of mind.

To strive for purity of vision, and yet be
blinded by faulty judgement – that prolongs
the bondage.

When a man knows the solitude of silence, and feels the joy of quietness, he is then free from fear and he feels the joy of the dharma.

One in All,
All in One –
if only this is realized,
no more worry about
you not being
perfect.

Material shape is not yours,
nor are feeling, perception,
the constructions or consciousness. These
are not yours. Put them away.

Not even the gods can turn
the victory of conquering oneself
into defeat.

Few cross the river of time and are able
to reach nirvana. Most of them run up
and down only on this side of the river.

When a fool does evil work, he forgets
that he is lighting a fire wherein he must
burn one day.

As rain penetrates an improperly shingled roof, so passion overwhelms a confused mind.

The perfect way knows no
difficulties except it refuses to
make preferences.

He who like the
moon is pure, bright,
clear and serene;
whose pleasure for things
that pass away –
him I call a Brahmin.

All beings and
everything – may they
all see luck, may
none come to evil.

He who is free from the
bondage of men and from the
bondage of the gods:
who is free of all things in creation –
him I call a Brahmin.

Who can trace the invisible path of the man who soars in the sky of liberation, the infinite Void without beginning, whose passions are peace, and over whom pleasure has no power? His path is as difficult to trace as that of the birds of the air.

He who is powerful, noble, who lives a life of inner heroism, the all-seer, the all-conqueror, the ever-pure, who has reached the end of his journey, who like the Buddha is awake – him I call a Brahmin.

A recluse's goal is patience and forbearance. Wisdom is his ambition, moral habit is his resolve, nothingness his want, nirvana is his fulfilment.

Since they have compassion
for him, as a mother
for her child, a man,
through the gods'
compassion, sees good
everywhere.

When beyond meditation and contemplation a Brahmin has reached the far shore, then he obtains the supreme vision and all his fetters are broken.

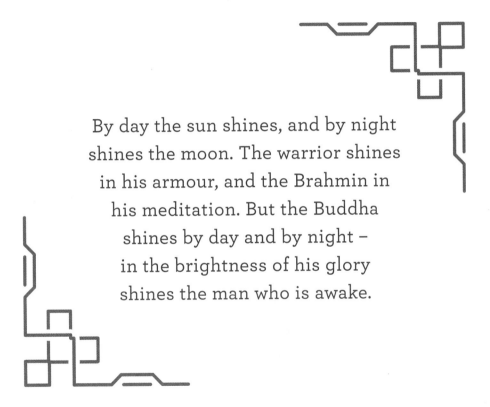

By day the sun shines, and by night
shines the moon. The warrior shines
in his armour, and the Brahmin in
his meditation. But the Buddha
shines by day and by night –
in the brightness of his glory
shines the man who is awake.

There are four bases
of sympathy: charity,
kind speech, doing a
good turn and treating
all alike.

Consumed by wisdom, faults cease to thrive and grow, like a tree which flares up after it has been struck by a thunderbolt.

Conquest engenders; the conquered lives
in misery. But who so is at peace and
passionless, happily doth he live; conquest
has he abandoned and defeat.

He who speaks words that
are peaceful and useful and
true, words that offend no one –
him I call a Brahmin.

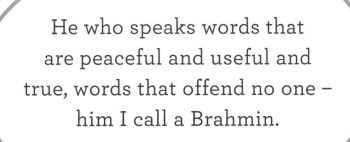

By entering on the eightfold path, which has morality, concentration and wisdom as its three divisions, and which is holy, incorruptible and straight, one forsakes those faults which are the cause of suffering and one attains the state of absolute peace.

This is the beginning of the life of
the wise monk; self-control
of the senses, happiness,
living under moral law, and whose
life is pure and who are ever striving.

He whose vision is deep, who is wise,
who knows the path and
what is outside the path, who has
attained the highest end –
him I call a Brahmin.

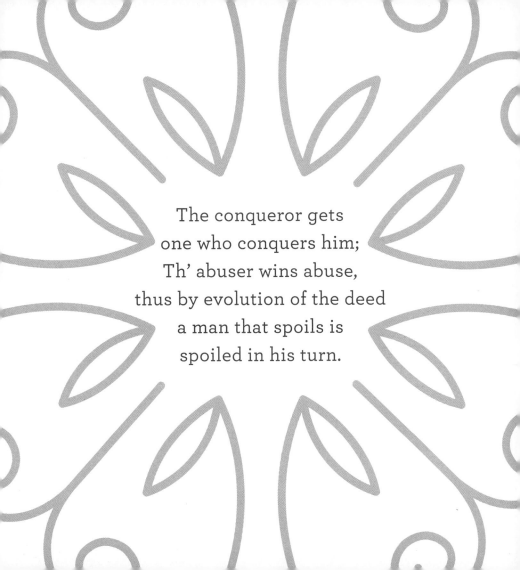

The conqueror gets
one who conquers him;
Th' abuser wins abuse,
thus by evolution of the deed
a man that spoils is
spoiled in his turn.

Let him no creatures kill
and none incite
to kill, nor sanction others
taking life, but put by violence
for all that lives.

He who in this world has
gone beyond good and
evil and both, who free
from sorrows is free
from passions and is pure
– him I call a Brahmin.

Easy to see are others' faults, those of self are hard to see. Surely the faults of other men a man doth winnow as 'twere chaff, but those of the self he covers up like a crafty gamester losing his throw.

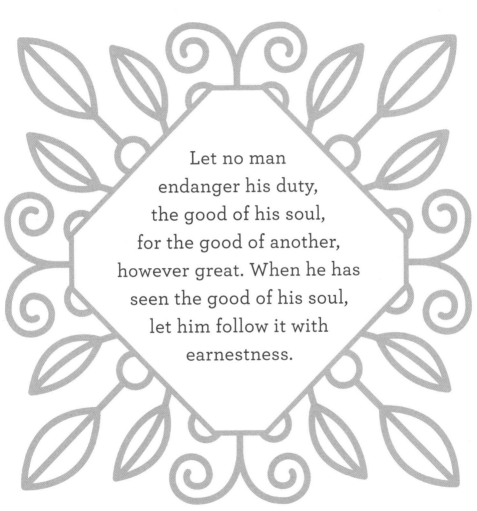

Let no man
endanger his duty,
the good of his soul,
for the good of another,
however great. When he has
seen the good of his soul,
let him follow it with
earnestness.

All material shapes, feelings, perceptions,
constructions, and all consciousness,
whether past, future or present, subjective or
objective, gross or subtle, mean or excellent,
near or far, must all be seen as:
this is not mine, I am not this, this is not myself.

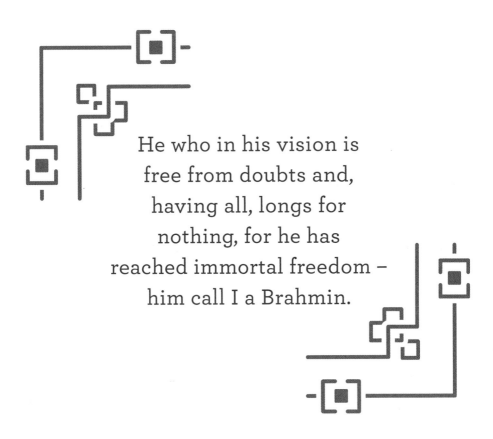

He who in his vision is free from doubts and, having all, longs for nothing, for he has reached immortal freedom – him call I a Brahmin.

If acts of thought are done through love
towards his fellows in the Brahma-faring,
both openly and in private – this is a matter
which conduces to unity.

Let him first find
what is right and then
he can teach it to
others, thus avoiding
useless pain.

There is not in the world an evil deed that lies hidden. The Self, O man, knows what of you is true or false. Ah, sir, the lovely Self you despise who in the small self hides the self that is evil.

Faith is the wealth here best
for man; dharma pursued
brings happiness;
and truth is sweet
beyond compare; life
wisely lived they say is best.

By faith the flood is crossed;
by earnestness the sea;
by vigour ill is passed;
by wisdom he is cleansed.

Freedom of heart that is love will
be made actual by us, made much of, made a
vehicle, made a basis, exercised, augmented
and thoroughly set going.

Ten qualities are
required of those who tread
the eightfold path: steadfastness,
sincerity, self-respect, vigilance,
seclusion from the world, contentment
with little, simplicity of tastes,
non-attachment, aversion of
worldly activity
and patience.

Abandoning the taking of what
is not given, abstaining from it,
the recluse Gautama lives as one
who takes only what is given,
who waits for it to be given;
not by stealing he lives
with Self become pure.

This contemplation is peaceful and excellent. It is for gaining tranquillity, for reaching one-pointed concentration. This knowledge is not in order to develop the habit of painful self denial.

You would like to possess
something that was
permanent, stable, eternal,
not liable to change,
that would stand fast like
unto the eternal.
But can you see such a
possession? Neither can I.

Who has bad
men as friends,
nor makes friends
with good, who
chooses men's bad
ways: a source of
suffering that.

Who fitly acts and toils
and strives shall riches find;
by trust shall fame acquire;
by giving, friends shall bind.

There are four bases of sympathy.
What four?
Charity, kind speech, doing good and
treating all alike.

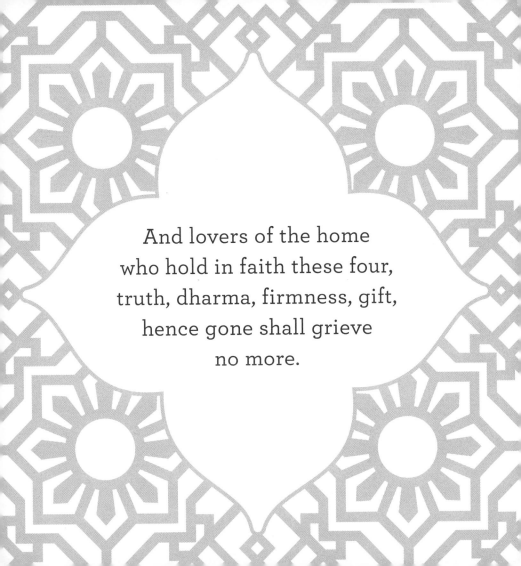

And lovers of the home
who hold in faith these four,
truth, dharma, firmness, gift,
hence gone shall grieve
no more.

Plain is the weal in life, plain is the suffering: prospers who dharma loves, suffers who dharma hates.

He who has virtue and vision, who follows
dharma, the Path of Perfection, whose words
are truth, and does the work to be done – the
world loves such a man.

You must slay anger if you
would live happily.
You must slay anger, if you
would weep no more.

Whatever wholesome dharmas there may be, they are all headed by concentration, they bend towards concentration, lead to concentration, incline to concentration.

He who has reached the yon
and nigh of things,
so all are ended, quenched
and no more, calm man,
and in attachment's
end released,
oblation-worthy is the
Man-thus-come.

He is not seen to come,
nor known to stay or go;
as signless and
motionless the supreme
Lord is known.

One who can recite many
sacred verses but cannot live
by them is like an accountant
who tallies the wealth of others.
He does not live in peace
and harmony.

The one steadfast,
released from views is
unsullied by the world,
not blamed by Self.

There is no fire
like lust, and no chains
like those of hate.
There is no net like
illusion and no rushing
torrent like desire.

Regarding body as body, feelings as feelings, thoughts as thoughts, mental states as mental states, control the hankering and dejection in this world.

Not to consider 'I am this,'
that is freedom.

In freedom
I am freed.

Seeing in what's impermanent the permanent, in what is ill what's well, in what is not-Self the Self, in what is ugly beauty, these are the erroneous views of the scatter-brained and unintelligent... They tread the round of becoming; theirs is the road of birth and death.

He is happy in his solitude who glad at heart has dharma learnt and the vision sees! Happy is that kindness towards the world; on no creature works harm.

And they who praise the blameworthy,
and they who blame the praiseworthy,
cull with the mouth the seeds of woe,
not from the seeds raise happiness.

This that is called thought and mind and consciousness, this by day and night dissolves as one thing and reappears as another. As a monkey passing through the jungle catches hold of a bough and having let it go, takes hold of another, even so that which is called thought and mind and consciousness, this by night and day dissolves as one thing and reappears as another.

A man is not called wise because he talks
and talks again; but if he is peaceful,
loving and fearless then he is in
truth called wise.

Creatures are heirs
to their deeds.

Do not trivialize small acts of peace and harmony, thinking, 'I will never reap what I have sown'. A pitcher is filled one drop of water at a time and a person centred in oneness who proceeds in peace and harmony will soon manifest the peace and harmony in his life.

If one abandons onslaught on creatures, abstains from it, lays aside stick, lays aside knife, he lives modest, merciful, compassionate towards all living creatures. He is not crooked in body, speech, thought.

He who destroys life,
who utters lies, who takes
what is not given to him,
who goes to the wife of another,
who gets drunk with strong
drinks – he digs up the
very roots of his life.

Not to be reached by locomotion
is World's End ever:
yet there is no release from ill
till it has been reached.
So let a man become a
World-knower,
World-ender, let him have
led the Brahma-faring –
knowing World's End,
as one pacified,
he longs not for this
or another world.

Go along having Self as lamp, Self as refuge and none other as refuge; having dharma as lamp, dharma as refuge and none other as refuge.

Formerly also, as well as now, all material shape was impermanent, suffering, liable to change. By right wisdom, seeing it thus as it really comes to be, sorrow, grief, lamentation and despair wane.

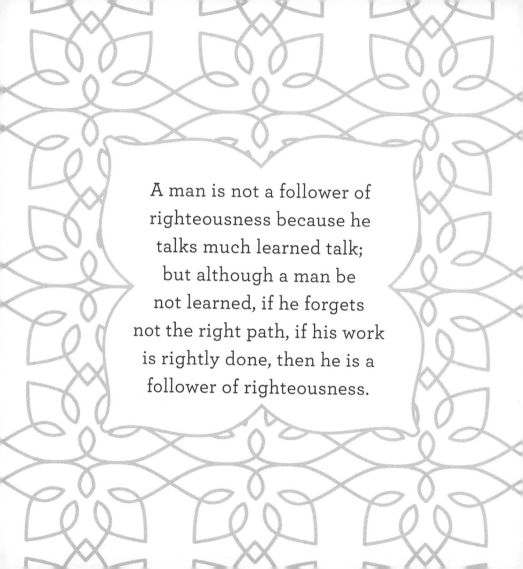

A man is not a follower of
righteousness because he
talks much learned talk;
but although a man be
not learned, if he forgets
not the right path, if his work
is rightly done, then he is a
follower of righteousness.

A man is not a great man because
he is a warrior and kills other men; but
because he hurts not any living being, he in
truth is called great man.

Material shape is like a ball of foam,
feelings like unto a bubble blown,
perceptions like a mirage are,
the constructions like a
plantain tree,
consciousness like an illusion:
so said the Kinsman of the Sun.

And what is right speech? Abstaining from lying, from divisive speech, from abusive speech, and from idle chatter: this is called right speech.

He should desire to pursue
neither extremes,
committing nothing that
the Self would blame.

Devas and Truth-seekers
see the fool walking unevenly
in the world; wherefore
let the 'master of himself'
walk recollectedly, heedfully,
contemplative.

The self is
not in Self.

The end remains untold.

Each of the Sayings was derived from the following Buddhist texts:

Anguttara-Nikaya
Bodhicaryavatara
Buddhacarita
Bya chos
Digha-Nikaya
Diamond Sutra
Digh-Nakaya
Dhammapada
Dohakosha
Doctrinal texts collected by C. Humphries
Itivuttka
Jatakamala
Majahima-Nikaya
Milindapanha
On Hakuin's Zazen Wasan
Papancasudani
Prajnaparamitastotrha
Samyuyutta-Nikaya
Sessan Amakuki
Sin sin ming
Sutanipata
Udana
Vinaya-Pitaka
Visuddhimagga

Arcturus Publishing Limited have made every reasonable effort to ensure that all permissions information has been sought and achieved as required. However there may be inadvertent and occasional errors in seeking permission to reproduce individual Sayings for which Arcturus Publishing Limited apologizes. If you are the Copyright owner of any such entry please contact Arcturus directly so we may add the necessary reference and acknowledgement.